Contents

DOUBLE HAPPINESS MOSAIC PILLOWS

Easy

MEASUREMENTS

Approx 18"/45.5cm square*

*will stretch to fit most 20"/51cm square pillow forms

MATERIALS

YARN

Any worsted-weight wool/mohair blend yarn, approx 4oz/113g and 190yd/174m per skein ⓪④⓪

• 4 skeins each in Cream (color 1), Navy (color 2), and Bright Blue (color 3)**

**4 skeins of each color will make all 3 pillows, a single pillow requires 2 skeins of each of 2 colors. Each color can be used as A or B according to the charts.

NEEDLES

• One pair each size 8 and 9 (5 and 5.5mm) needles, *or size to obtain gauge*

Notions

• Three 1½"/38mm buttons for each pillow

• Three 20"/51cm square pillow forms

• Stitch markers

GAUGE

18 sts and 34 rows to 4"/10cm over charts using larger needles. *TAKE TIME TO CHECK YOUR GAUGE.*

MOSAIC KNITTING

1) One row of chart represents 2 rows of knitting, a RS row and a WS row. Read RS rows from right to left and WS rows from left to right. Only one color is worked over 2 rows, the sts in the other color are slipped.

2) Chart is worked in garter st (k every row). The letters along right side of chart represent the color used to knit the row, and also correspond to the first and last st of the row. The other color will be slipped on those 2 rows.

3) All sts are slipped purlwise with the yarn at the WS of the work. Therefore, on RS rows sts are slipped wyib and on WS rows sts are slipped wyif.

4) When slipping 2 or more stitches, spread them out on RH needle and carry the yarn loosely across the back before working next st to avoid puckering.

5) For ease in knitting, place markers between chart reps.

PILLOW

With smaller needles and A, cast on 83 sts.

Knit 5 rows.

Buttonhole row (RS) K17, [bind off 5 sts, k16]
3 times.

Next row Knit, casting on 5 sts over each set of
bound-off sts.

Change to larger needles.

BEGIN CHART

Row 1 (RS) Work first st of chart, work 16-st rep
5 times, work last 2 sts of chart.

Cont to work chart in this way until 38 rows of chart
have been worked 8 times.

Change to smaller needles.

With A, work in garter st (k every row) for 3"/7.5cm
for buttonband. Bind off.

KNITTED BUTTON COVERS

(make 3 for each pillow)

With A, cast on 6 sts.

Knit 1 row, purl 1 row.

Inc row (RS) K1, M1, k to last st, M1, k1—2 sts inc'd.

Purl 1 row.

Rep last 2 rows twice more—12 sts.

Knit 1 row. Purl 1 row.

Dec row (RS) K1, k2tog, k to last 3 sts, ssk, k1—2 sts
dec'd.

Purl 1 row.

Rep last 2 rows twice more—6 sts.

Bind off.

Thread yarn around edge of button cover, place button
in middle of cover, pull yarn and sew edges tog.

FINISHING

Fold cast-on and bound-off edges so that four
complete chart reps form front of pillow. Bring edges
tog at center back of pillow. Sew buttons to garter
buttonband to correspond to buttonholes.

Sew side seams, overlapping buttonhole band over
buttonband.

Insert pillow form and button closed. •

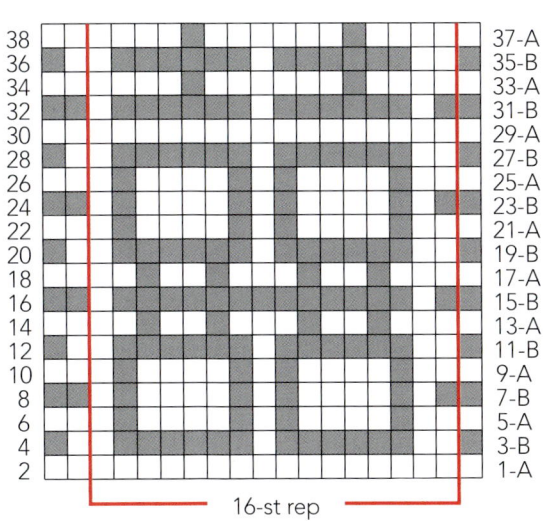

COLOR KEY

☐ A

▨ B

16-st rep

MOSAIC BABY BLANKET

Easy

MEASUREMENTS
Approx 30 x 31"/76 x 79cm

MATERIALS
YARN
Any DK-weight superwash wool yarn, approx 1¾oz/50g and 136yd/125m per skein **③**
• 6 skeins in Denim (A)
• 2 skeins in Baby Blue (B)
• 3 skeins in White (C)

NEEDLES
• One size 6 (4mm) circular needle, 24"/60cm long, *or size to obtain gauge*

GAUGE
24 sts and 50 rows to 4"/10cm over chart using size 6 (4mm) needles. *TAKE TIME TO CHECK YOUR GAUGE.*

MOSAIC KNITTING
1) One row of chart represents 2 rows of knitting, a RS row and a WS row. Read RS rows from right to left and WS rows from left to right. Only one color is worked over 2 rows, the sts in the other color are slipped.
2) Chart is worked in garter st (k every row). The letters along right side of chart represent color used to knit row, and also correspond to the first and last st of the row. The other color will be slipped on those 2 rows.
3) All sts are slipped purlwise with the yarn at the WS of the work. Therefore, on RS rows sts are slipped wyib and on WS rows sts are slipped wyif.
4) When slipping 2 or more stitches, spread them out on RH needle and carry the yarn loosely across the back before working next st to avoid puckering.

NOTES
1) Carry A along edge throughout. Cut B and C when blocks of color are finished and rejoin when needed.
2) Circular needle is used to accommodate the large number of stitches. Do not join.

BLANKET
PILLOW POCKET
With A, cast on 63 sts. Knit 3 rows.

Begin chart
Row 1 (RS) Work to rep line, work 12-st rep 4 times, work to end of chart.
Work chart in this way until 60 rows of chart have been worked twice, then work rows 1–26 once more.
With A, knit 3 rows. Bind off.

Side edging
With RS facing and A, pick up and k 1 st in every other row along side edge. Knit 3 rows. Bind off.
Rep for rem side edge.

BLANKET
With A, cast on 171 sts. Knit 3 rows.

Begin chart
Row 1 (RS) Work to rep line, work 12-st rep 13 times, work to end of chart.
Work chart in this way until 60 rows of chart have been worked 6 times, then work rows 1–26 once more.
With A, knit 3 rows. Bind off.

Side edging
With RS facing and A, pick up and k 1 st in every other row along side edge. Knit 3 rows. Bind off.
Rep for rem side edge.

MOSAIC BABY BLANKET

FINISHING

With RS of pocket facing WS of blanket and with pocket centered, sew bound-off edge of pocket along bound-off edge of blanket. Sew bottom and sides of pocket in place. •

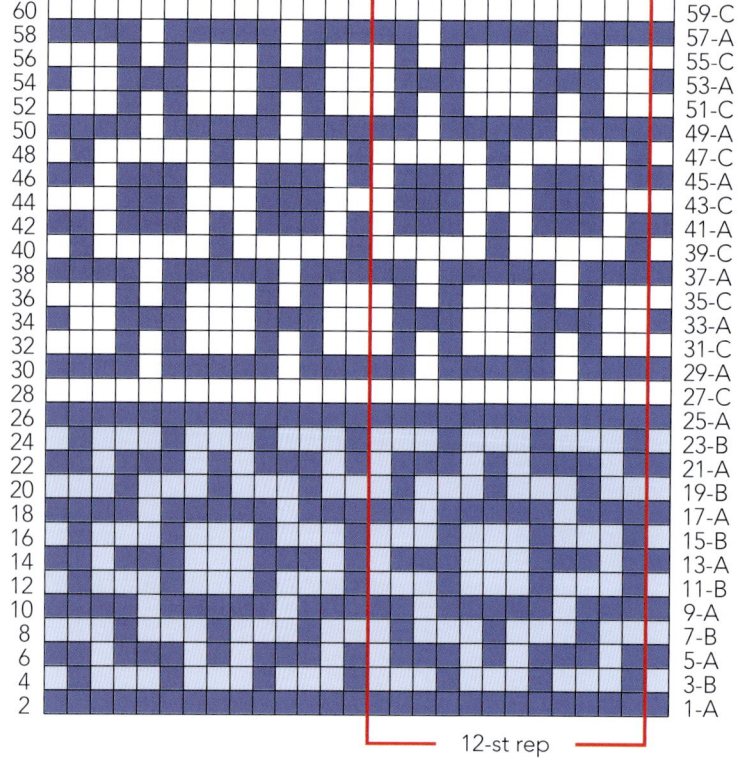

COLOR KEY

- A
- B
- C

12-st rep

FOLDING TUTORIAL

1) Shown here is the finished blanket from the right side.

2) The pocket is sewn to the wrong side of the blanket along three sides, in the center of the top edge, shown above.

3) To fold the blanket into a pillow, lay the blanket with the right side facing. Fold the right third over the center, as shown.

4) Fold the left third of the blanket over the center.

5) Fold the lower third of the blanket up toward the pocket, as shown, then fold in half with the pocket side down.

6) Reach into the pocket, grasping the folded blanket, and turn the pocket inside out.

7) The result? A comfy pillow and a neat way to store the blanket.

MITERED SQUARES BLANKET

Easy

MEASUREMENTS

Approx 39"/99cm square

MATERIALS

YARN

Any bulky-weight wool/mohair blend yarn, approx 4oz/113g and 125yd/114m per skein **(5)**

• 6 skeins in Light Brown (A)

• 2 skeins in Charcoal (B)

• 1 skein in Aran (C)

NEEDLES

• One pair size 10½ (6.5mm) needles, *or size to obtain gauge*

NOTIONS

• Stitch markers

GAUGE

11 sts and 22 rows to 4"/10cm over garter st using size 10½ (6.5mm) needles. *TAKE TIME TO CHECK YOUR GAUGE.*

NOTE

Use diagram and photo as guide when picking up adjacent squares.

BLANKET

SQUARE 1

With A, cast on 73 sts.

Row 1 (RS) K35, SK2P, k35—2 sts dec'd.

Row 2 Knit.

Row 3 K34, SK2P, k34—2 sts dec'd.

Row 4 Knit.

Cont in this way, working 1 st less before center double decrease every other row, until 1 st rem. Fasten off last st.

SQUARE 2

With RS facing and A, pick up and k 36 sts along left side edge of square 1, cast on 37 sts—73 sts. Knit 1 row. Complete as for square 1.

SQUARE 3

With A, cast on 37 sts, then with RS facing, pick up and k 36 sts along upper edge of square 1—73 sts. Knit 1 row. Complete as for square 1.

SQUARE 4

With RS facing and B, pick up and k 36 sts along left edge of square 2, then cast on 37 sts—73 sts. Knit 1 row. Complete as for square 1.

SQUARE 5

With RS facing and C, pick up and k 36 sts along left edge of square 3, pick up and k 1 st in corner, pick up and k 36 sts along upper edge of square 2—73 sts. Knit 1 row. Complete as for square 1.

SQUARE 6

With B, cast on 37 sts, then with RS facing, pick up and k 36 sts along upper edge of square 3—73 sts. Knit 1 row. Complete as for square 1.

SQUARE 7

With RS facing and A, pick up and k 36 sts along left edge of square 5, pick up and k 1 st in corner, pick up and k 36 sts along upper edge of square 4—73 sts. Knit 1 row. Complete as for square 1.

SQUARE 8

With RS facing and A, pick up and k 36 sts along left edge of square 6, pick up and k 1 st in corner, pick up and k 36 sts along upper edge of square 5—73 sts.
Knit 1 row. Complete as for square 1.

SQUARE 9

With RS facing and A, pick up and k 36 sts along left edge of square 8, pick up and k 1 st in corner, pick up and k 36 sts along upper edge of square 7—73 sts.
Knit 1 row. Complete as for square 1.

FINISHING

Weave in ends. Block lightly to measurements. •

COLOR KEY
A
B
C

TEXTURED PILLOW DUO

SQUARE PILLOW

MEASUREMENTS

Approx 18"/45.5cm*

*will stretch to fit most 20"/51cm square pillow forms

MATERIALS

YARN

Any super bulky-weight wool yarn, approx 3½oz/100g and 54yd/49m per skein

• 2 skeins each in Light Brown (A) and Aran (B)

• 3 skeins in Charcoal (C)

NEEDLES

• One pair size 15 (10mm) needles, *or size to obtain gauge*

NOTION

• One 20"/51cm square pillow form

GAUGE

8 sts and 14 rows to 4"/10cm over seed st using size 15 (10mm) needles. TAKE TIME TO CHECK YOUR GAUGE.

SEED STITCH

(over an even number of sts)

Row 1 *K1, p1; rep from * to end.

Row 2 *P1, k1; rep from * to end.

Rep rows 1 and 2 for seed st.

DOUBLE SEED STITCH

(over an even number of sts)

Rows 1 and 2 *K1, p1; rep from * to end.

Rows 3 and 4 *P1, k1; rep from * to end.

Rep rows 1–4 for double seed st.

NOTE

When changing colors, twist yarns on WS to prevent holes in work.

RIDGE PATTERN

Row 1 (RS) Knit.

Row 2 Purl.

Rows 3 and 4 Knit.

Rep rows 1–4 for ridge pat.

COVER

With A, cast on 18 sts; with C, cast on 18 sts—36 sts.

Row 1 (RS) With C, work in seed st over 18 sts; with A, work in double seed st over 18 sts.

Cont in pats as established, working A sts in A and C sts in C, for 31 rows more, end with a WS row. Cut A and C.

Next row (RS) With B, k18; with C, k18.

Next row With C, work in seed st over 18 sts; with B, work ridge pat over 18 sts beg with row 2.

Cont in pats as established, working B sts in B and C sts in C, for 30 rows more, end with a WS row. Cut B and C.

Next row (RS) With C, k18, with B, k18.

Next row With B, work ridge pat over 18 sts beg with row 2, with C, work in seed st over 18 sts.

Cont in pats as established, working C sts in C and B sts in B, for 30 rows more, end with a WS row. Cut B and C.

Next row (RS) With A, k18, with C, k18.

Next row With C, work in seed st over 18 sts, with A, work in double seed st over 18 sts.

Cont in pats as established, working A sts in A and C sts in C, for 30 rows more, end with a WS row. Bind off.

FINISHING

Weave in ends. Block lightly to measurements.

Fold cover in half and sew side seams. Insert pillow form and sew closed. •

TEXTURED PILLOW DUO

RECTANGULAR PILLOW

MEASUREMENTS

Approx 11 x 18"/28 x 45.5cm*

*will stretch to fit most 12 x 20"/30.5 x 51cm pillow forms

MATERIALS

YARN

Any super bulky-weight wool yarn, approx 3½oz/100g and 54yd/49m per skein

- 2 skeins in Light Brown (A)
- 1 skein each in Aran (B) and Charcoal (C)

NEEDLES

- One pair size 15 (10mm) needles, *or size to obtain gauge*

NOTION

- One 12 x 20"/30.5 x 51cm pillow form

GAUGE

8 sts and 12 rows to 4"/10cm over St st using size 15 (10mm) needles. *TAKE TIME TO CHECK YOUR GAUGE.*

PILLOW

SECTION 1

With A, cast on 49 sts.

Row 1 (RS) K1, *p1, k1; rep from * to end.

Row 2 P1, *k1, p1; rep from * to end.

Row 3 Knit.

Row 4 Purl.

Rep rows 1–4 twice more. Cut A.

SECTION 2

Join B. [Knit 3 rows, purl 1 row] twice, knit 2 rows.

SECTION 3

Cut B. Join C.

Next row (RS) Knit.

Next row K1, *p1, k1; rep from * to end.

Rep last row for seed st for 14 rows more. Cut C.

SECTION 4

Work as for section 2.

SECTION 5

Join A.

Row 1 (RS) Knit.

Row 2 Purl.

Row 3 K1, *p1, k1; rep from * to end.

Row 4 P1, *k1, p1; rep from * to end.

Rep rows 1–4 twice more.

Bind off.

FINISHING

Weave in ends. Block lightly to measurements.

Fold cover in half lengthwise and sew side seams. Insert pillow form and sew closed. •

STRIPED PILLOW

Easy

MEASUREMENTS

18"/45.5cm square

MATERIALS

YARN

Any super bulky-weight wool, approx 7oz/200g and 175yd/160m per skein **6**

• 1 skein each in Blue (A), White (B), and Green (C)

NEEDLES

• One pair size 13 (9mm) needles, *or size to obtain gauge*

• One extra size 13 (9mm) needle

NOTIONS

• One 18"/45.5cm square pillow form

GAUGE

11 sts and 16 rows to 4"/10cm in St st using size 13 (9mm) needles. *TAKE TIME TO CHECK YOUR GAUGE.*

BACK

With A, cast on 50 sts.

Beg with a knit (RS) row, work in St st (k on RS, p on WS) for 10"/25.5cm, end with a WS row. Cut A.

Join B and work 10 rows in St st. Cut B. Join C.

Next row (RS) Knit.

Next row (WS) P2, *k2, p2; rep from * to end.

Rep last 2 rows until piece measures 18"/45.5cm from beg, end with a WS row.

Leave sts on spare needle.

FRONT

Work as for back, leaving sts on needle.

FINISHING

Weave in ends. Block pieces to measurements.

Seam 3 edges of front and back tog. Insert pillow form and sew cast-on edges closed. •

STRIPED THROW

Easy

MEASUREMENTS

Approx 45½ x 56"/113 x 142cm

MATERIALS

YARN

Any super bulky-weight wool yarn, approx 7oz/200g and 175yd/160m per skein

• 2 skeins each in White (A) and Blue (B)

• 3 skeins in Green (C)

NEEDLES

• One size 15 (10mm) circular needle, 32"/80cm long, *or size to obtain gauge*

GAUGE

10½ sts and 15 rows to 4"/10cm in garter rib using size 15 (10mm) needles. *TAKE TIME TO CHECK YOUR GAUGE.*

NOTE

Circular needle is used to accommodate the large number of stitches. Do not join.

GARTER RIB

(over an odd number of sts)

Row 1 (WS) K1, *p1, k1; rep from * to end.

Row 2 Knit.

Rep rows 1 and 2 for garter rib.

THROW

With A, cast on 117 sts.

Beg with a WS row, work in garter rib for 8"/20.5cm, end with a WS row. Cut A

Join B and work in garter rib for 4"/10cm, end with a WS row. Cut B.

Join A and work in garter rib for 8"/20.5cm, end with a WS row. Cut A.

Join B and work in garter rib for 4"/10cm, end with a WS row. Cut B.

Join C and work in garter rib for 12"/30.5cm, end with a WS row. Cut C.

Join B and work in garter rib for 8"/20.5cm, end with a WS row. Cut B.

Join C and work in garter rib for 12"/30.5cm, end with a RS row.

Bind off all sts loosely in pat.

FINISHING

Weave in ends. Block to measurements. •

GINGERBREAD LACE BLANKET

MEASUREMENTS

Approx 36 x 49"/90 x 124cm

MATERIALS

YARN

Any bulky-weight baby alpaca yarn, approx 3½oz/100g and 110yd/100m per skein

• 9 skeins in Light Green

NEEDLES

• One pair each size 10 and 10½ (6 and 6.5mm) needles, *or size to obtain gauge*

GAUGE

12 sts and 18 rows to 4"/10cm over lace pat using larger needles. *TAKE TIME TO CHECK YOUR GAUGE.*

GINGERBREAD LACE PATTERN

(begin and end with a multiple of 6 sts plus 9)

Note The st rep alternates between 6 and 8 sts.

Row 1 (RS) K4, *k1, yo, SKP, k1, k2tog, yo; rep from * to last 5 sts, k5.

Row 2 and every WS row K3, p to last 3 sts, k3.

Row 3 K4, *k2, yo, k3, yo, k1; rep from * to last 5 sts, k5.

Row 5 K4, k2tog, *yo, SKP, k1, k2tog, yo, SK2P; rep from * to last 11 sts, yo, SKP, k1, k2tog, yo, SKP, k4.

Row 7 K4, *k1, k2tog, yo, k1, yo, SKP; rep from * to last 5 sts, k5.

Row 9 Rep row 3.

Row 11 K4, *k1, k2tog, yo, SK2P, yo, SKP; rep from * to last 5 sts, k5.

Row 12 K3, p to last 3 sts, k3.

Rep rows 1–12 for gingerbread lace pat.

BLANKET

With smaller needles, cast on 111 sts.

Work 10 rows in garter st (k every row).

Next row Knit.

Next row K3, p to last 3 sts, k3.

Change to larger needles and work in gingerbread lace pat until blanket measures approx 47"/120cm, end with a pat row 12.

Change to smaller needles.

Work 10 rows in garter st. Bind off.

FINISHING

Weave in ends. Block to measurements. •

PAILLETTE CABLES PILLOW

Intermediate

MEASUREMENTS
20"/51cm square

MATERIALS

YARN
Any worsted-weight wool yarn, approx 3½oz/100g and 218yd/199m per skein ⓸
• 4 skeins in Cornflower Blue

NEEDLES
• One pair size 7 (4.5mm) needles, *or size to obtain gauge*

NOTIONS
• Two cable needles (cn)
• One 20"/51cm square pillow form

GAUGE
21 sts and 29 rows to 4"/10cm in St st using size 7 (4.5mm) needles. *TAKE TIME TO CHECK YOUR GAUGE.*

STITCH GLOSSARY
11-st Cross Sl 4 sts to first cn and hold to back, sl next 3 sts to 2nd cn and hold to front, k4, k3 from 2nd cn, k4 from first cn.

NOTE
Cable pat can be worked from instructions or chart.

CABLE PATTERN
(multiple of 28 sts plus 5)

Row 1 (RS) P4, *k11, p3; rep from * to last st, p1.
Row 2 and all WS rows K1, *k3, p11; rep from * to last 4 sts, k4.
Rows 3, 5, 7, and 9 P4, *k11, p3; rep from * to last st, p1.
Row 11 P4, *k11, p3, 11-st cross, p3; rep from * to last st, p1.
Rows 13, 15, 17, and 19 Rep row 3.
Row 21 P4, *11-st cross, p3, k11, p3; rep from * to last st, p1.
Rep rows 2–21 for cable pat.

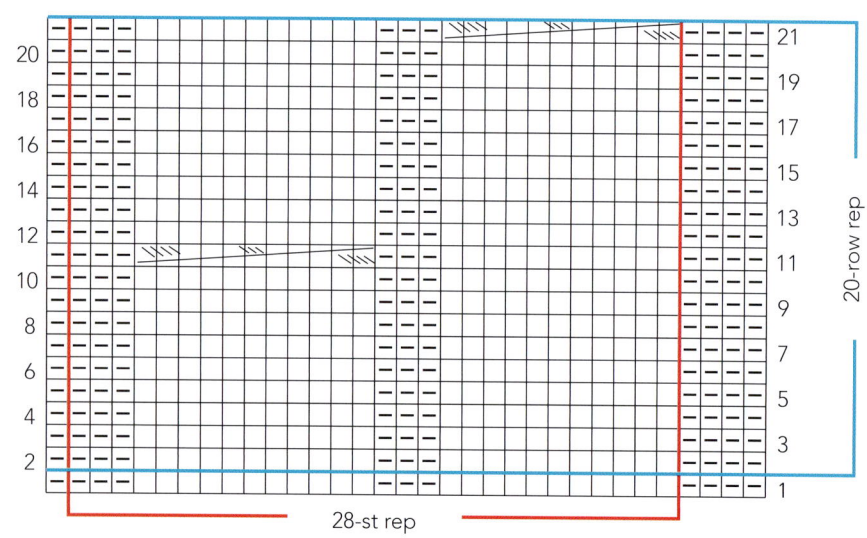

STITCH KEY
☐ k on RS, p on WS
⊟ p on RS, k on WS
⟍⟍ 11-st Cross

PILLOWS

BACK

Cast on 107 sts. Work in reverse St st (p on RS, k on WS) until piece measures 20"/51cm from beg, end with a WS row. Bind off all sts.

FRONT

Cast on 125 sts.

Row 1 (RS) P4, [k11, p3, k7, p3] 5 times, p1.

Inc row 2 K4, *[p1, M1 p-st] twice, p3, [M1 p-st, p1] twice, k3, p11, k3; rep from* to last st, k1—145 sts.

Begin cable pattern

Row (RS) Work row 3 of cable pat to end of row.

Cont in cable pat, working through row 21, then rep rows 2–21 five times more, then rows 2–9 once more.

Next dec row (WS) K4, *[p2tog] twice, p3, [p2tog] twice, k3, p11, k3; rep from * to last st, k1—125 sts. Bind off all sts.

FINISHING

Weave in ends. Block pieces to measurements. Sew 3 sides of pillow tog. Insert pillow form and sew 4th side closed. •

GEOMETRIC ILLUSION PILLOW

Easy

MEASUREMENTS

20"/51cm square

MATERIALS

YARN

Any worsted-weight superwash merino yarn, 3½oz/100g and 218yd/199m per skein ④

• 4 skeins in Seafoam Green

NEEDLES

• One pair size 7 (4.5mm) needles, *or size to obtain gauge*

NOTIONS

• One 20"/51cm square pillow form

GAUGE

22½ sts and 29 rows to 4"/10cm in geometric illusion pat (slightly stretched) using size 7 (4.5mm) needles. *TAKE TIME TO CHECK YOUR GAUGE.*

NOTE

Geometric illusion pattern can be worked from written instructions or chart.

GEOMETRIC ILLUSION PATTERN

(multiple of 18 sts plus 6)

Rows 1 and 3 (RS) Knit.

Rows 2 and 4 Purl.

Rows 5, 7, and 9 K1, *k13, p5; rep from * to last 5 sts, k5.

Rows 6, 8, and 10 P5, *k5, p13; rep from * to last st, p1.

Rows 11, 13, and 15 Knit.

Rows 12, 14, and 16 Purl.

Rows 17, 19, and 21 K1, *k4, p5, k9; rep from * to last 5 sts, k5.

Rows 18, 20, and 22 P5, *p9, k5, p4; rep from * to last st, p1.

Row 23 Knit.

Row 24 Purl.

Rep rows 1–24 for geometric illusion pat.

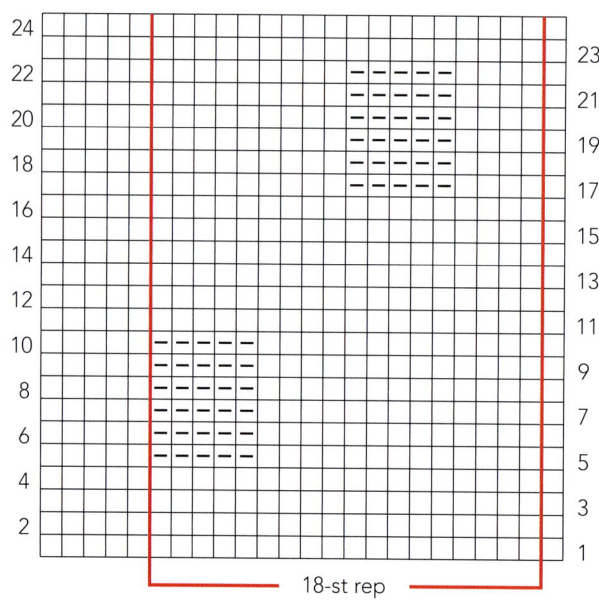

18-st rep

STITCH KEY

☐ k on RS, p on WS

⊟ p on RS, k on WS

PILLOW

Cast on 114 sts.

Beg with row 1, work in geometric illusion pat until
piece measures 20"/51cm from beg, end with a WS row.
Bind off.

Rep from beg for opposite side.

FINISHING

Weave in ends. Block to measurements.

Sew 3 sides of pillow together. Insert pillow form and
sew 4th side closed. •

SMOCKED BLANKET

Easy

MEASUREMENTS

Approx 49 x 55"/124.5 x 140cm*

*measurements do not include fringe

MATERIALS

YARN

Any bulky-weight wool yarn, approx 3½oz/100g and 110yd/101m per skein (**5**)

• 18 skeins in White

NEEDLES

• One pair size 15 (10mm) needles, *or size to obtain gauge*

GAUGE

13.25 sts and 14 rows to 4"/10cm over smocking st using size 15 (10mm) needles. *TAKE TIME TO CHECK YOUR GAUGE.*

NOTE

Blanket is knit in three separate panels, two side panels and one center panel, then seamed together.

SMOCKING STITCH

(multiple of 8 sts plus 2)

Row 1 (RS) P2, *k2, p2; rep from * to end.

Row 2 and all WS rows K2, *p2, k2; rep from * to end.

Row 3 P2, *bring yarn to back, insert RH needle from front between 6th and 7th sts on LH needle, draw loop through; sl this loop onto LH needle and knit it tog with first st on LH needle; k1, p2, k2, p2; rep from * to end.

Row 5 Rep row 1.

Row 7 P2, k2, p2, *bring yarn to back, draw loop as before and knit it tog with first st on LH needle; then k1, p2, k2, p2; rep from * to last 4 sts, k2, p2.

Row 8 K2, *p2, k2; rep from * to end.

Rep rows 1–8 for smocking st.

INVISIBLE SEAMING

Worked on reverse St st from the RS. Place the pieces to be joined on a flat surface with the RS facing. Begin at the lower edge, insert tapestry needle under the bottom loop of a purl stitch on one side of the seam, and then under the top loop of the corresponding purl stitch on the opposite side. Pull yarn through, tightening the seam just enough to merge the two pieces. Continue to alternate from side to side in every stitch.

BLANKET

SIDE PANELS (MAKE 2)

Cast on 50 sts.

Row 1 (RS) P2, *k2, p2; rep from * to end.

Row and all WS rows K2, *p2, k2; rep from * to end.

Rep last 2 rows for k2, p2 rib twice more.

Begin smocking stitch

Next row (RS) Rib 12 sts as established, work row 1 of smocking st over next 26 sts, rib 12 sts as established.

Next row Rib 12, work row 2 of smocking st, rib 12.

Cont in pats as established until 8 rows of smocking st have been worked 22 times, then work rows 1–4 once more.

Cont rib over all sts for 6 rows. Bind off in rib.

CENTER PANEL

Cast on 66 sts.

Work in k2, p2 rib as for side panel for 6 rows.

SMOCKED BLANKET

Begin smocking stitch

Work in smocking st over all sts until 8 rows of smocking st have been worked 22 times, then work rows 1–4 once more.

Cont rib over all sts for 6 rows. Bind off in rib.

FINISHING

Weave in ends. Block to measurements.

Seam panels tog using invisible seaming.

FRINGE

Cut 120 strands each 16"/40.5cm long. Using 3 strands for each fringe, attach a fringe in the center of each k2 rib along cast-on and bound-off edges. •

LATTICE PILLOWS

Easy

MEASUREMENTS

18"/46.5cm square

MATERIALS

Yarn

Any super bulky-weight acrylic/wool blend yarn, approx 6oz/170g and 106yd/97m per skein **6**

• 6 skeins in Aran

NEEDLES

• One pair size 15 (10mm) needles, *or size to obtain gauge*

NOTIONS

• Two 18"/46cm square pillow forms

• Removable stitch marker

• Lighter weight yarn in similar color for seaming

• One 4"/10cm piece of cardboard (optional, for tassels)

GAUGE

9 sts and 12 rows to 4"/10cm over St st using size 15 (10mm) needles. *TAKE TIME TO CHECK GAUGE.*

NOTE

Lattice pat can worked from written instructions or chart.

LATTICE PILLOWS

STITCH GLOSSARY

2-st RT K2tog without slipping sts off LH needle, then knit into first st again and slip both sts off needle.

2-st LT With RH needle behind LH needle, skip next st and knit 2nd st tbl; then insert RH needle into backs of both sts and k2tog tbl.

LATTICE PATTERN

(multiple of 8 sts plus 10)

Row 1 and all WS rows Purl.

Row 2 K1, *2-st LT, k4, 2-st RT; rep from * to last st, k1.

Row 4 K1, *k1, 2-st LT, k2, 2-st RT, k1; rep from * to last st, k1.

Row 6 K1, *k2, 2-st LT, 2-st RT, k2; rep from * to last st, k1.

Row 8 K1, *k3, 2-st RT, k3; rep from * to last st, k1.

Row 10 K1, *k2, 2-st RT, 2-st LT, k2; rep from * to last st, k1.

Row 12 K1, *k1, 2-st RT, k2, 2-st LT, k1; rep from * to last st, k1.

Row 14 K1, *2-st RT, k4, 2-st LT; rep from * to last st, k1.

Row 16 K2, *k6, 2-st LT; rep from * to last 8 sts, k8.

Rep rows 1–16 for lattice pat.

PILLOW

FRONT

Cast on 42 sts. Work rows 1–16 of lattice pat 3 times.

Work rows 1–8 once more.

Bind off knitwise.

BACK (MAKE 2)

Cast on 42 sts.

Next row (RS) K1, *k2, p2; rep from * to last st, k1.

Next 3 rows K the knit sts and p the purl sts.

Beg with a knit (RS) row, work in St st (k on RS, p on WS) until piece measures 10"/25.5cm from beg. Bind off.

FINISHING

Align one back panel to front with ribbing towards center of pillow, WS held tog. Seam back panel to front along outer edges. Align 2nd back panel, overlapping the first by 1"/2.5cm. Seam 2nd back panel to front along outer edges.

TASSEL (OPTIONAL, MAKE 4)

Wrap yarn around 4"/10cm piece of cardboard, leaving a 12"/30cm strand loose at either end. With a yarn needle, knot both sides to the first loop and run the loose strand under the wrapped strands. Pull tightly and tie at the top. Cut the lower edge of the tassel and, holding the tassel about ¾"/2cm from the top, wind the top strands (one clockwise and one counterclockwise) around the tassel. Thread the two strands and insert them through the top of the tassel.

Secure one tassel to each corner.

Insert pillow form. •

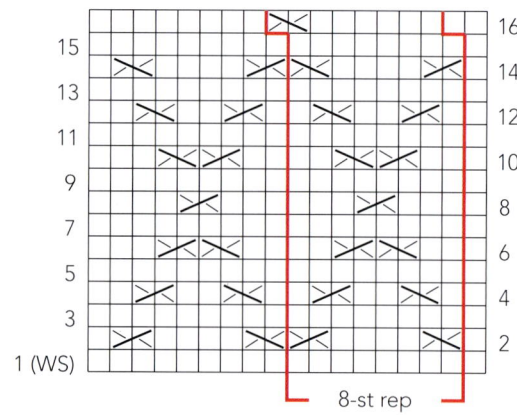

STITCH KEY

☐   k on RS, p on WS

⧖   2-st RT

⧗   2-st LT

STRIPED LOG CABIN AFGHAN & PILLOW SET

Easy

MEASUREMENTS

Afghan Approx 46 x 55"/117 x 140cm

Pillow 18"/46cm square

MATERIALS

YARN

Any aran-weight superwash yarn, approx 3½oz/100g and 220yd/200m per skein (4)

Afghan

• 5 skeins in Light Gray (A)

• 4 skeins in Charcoal (B)

• 3 skeins in Turquoise (C)

Pillows

• 2 skeins in Silver Gray (A)

• 1 skeins in Charcoal (B)

• 1 skeins in Turquoise (C)

NEEDLES

• One size 10 (6mm) circular needle, 32"/80cm long, *or size to obtain gauge*

NOTIONS

• Two 18"/46cm square pillow forms

• Two 18"/46cm square pieces of felt fabric

GAUGES

16 sts and 32 rows to 4"/10cm over garter st using size 10 (6mm) needle. *TAKE TIME TO CHECK YOUR GAUGE.*

NOTES

1) See afghan diagram on page 30.

2) Weave in ends as you go to minimize finishing.

AFGHAN

SECTION 1

With A, cast on 80 sts.

Work in garter st (k every row) for 102 rows. Cut A.

Join B. Cont in garter st for 104 rows. Cut B.

Join A. Cont in garter st for 103 rows.

Bind off knitwise on WS.

SECTION 2

Turn work 90 degrees counter clockwise. With RS facing and B, pick up and k 1 st in each garter ridge along side edge of Section 1—156 sts.

With B, work garter st for 27 rows. Cut B.

Join A, cont in garter st for 28 rows. Cut A.

Join B. cont in garter st for 28 rows. Cut B.

Join A, cont in garter st for 28 rows. Cut A.

Join C. Cont in garter st for 27 rows. Bind off knitwise WS.

SECTION 3

Rep as for Section 2 on opposite side edge of Section 1.

SECTION 4

With RS facing and C, pick up and k 1 st in each garter ridge along side of Section 2, 1 st from each st along top edge of Section 1, and 1 st in each garter ridge along side edge of Section 3—220 sts.

Work in garter st for 26 rows. Bind off knitwise on WS.

SECTION 5

Rep as for Section 4 on opposite side edge.

FINISHING

Weave in ends. Block to measurements.

STRIPED LOG CABIN AFGHAN & PILLOW SET

PILLOWS

SECTION 1

With A, cast on 26 sts.

Work in garter st (k every row) for 48 rows. Cut A.

Join B. Cont in garter st for 48 rows. Cut B.

Join A, cont in garter st for 49 rows. Bind off knitwise on WS.

SECTION 2

Turn work 90 degrees counter clockwise. With RS facing and B, pick up and k 1 st in each garter ridge along side edge of Section 1—72 sts.

With B, work in garter st for 16 rows. Cut B.

Join A. Cont in garter st for 16 rows. Cut A.

Join C. Cont in garter st for 17 rows. Bind off knitwise on WS.

SECTION 3

Rotate work 180 degrees and rep as for Section 2 along opposite side edge of Section 1.

FINISHING

Weave in ends. Block to measurements.

Sew 18"/46cm square felt piece to knitted piece, leaving one side open. Insert pillow form and sew rem side.

Note The pillow in the photo was made with a felt backing. If desired, the backing can be knit the same as the front. •

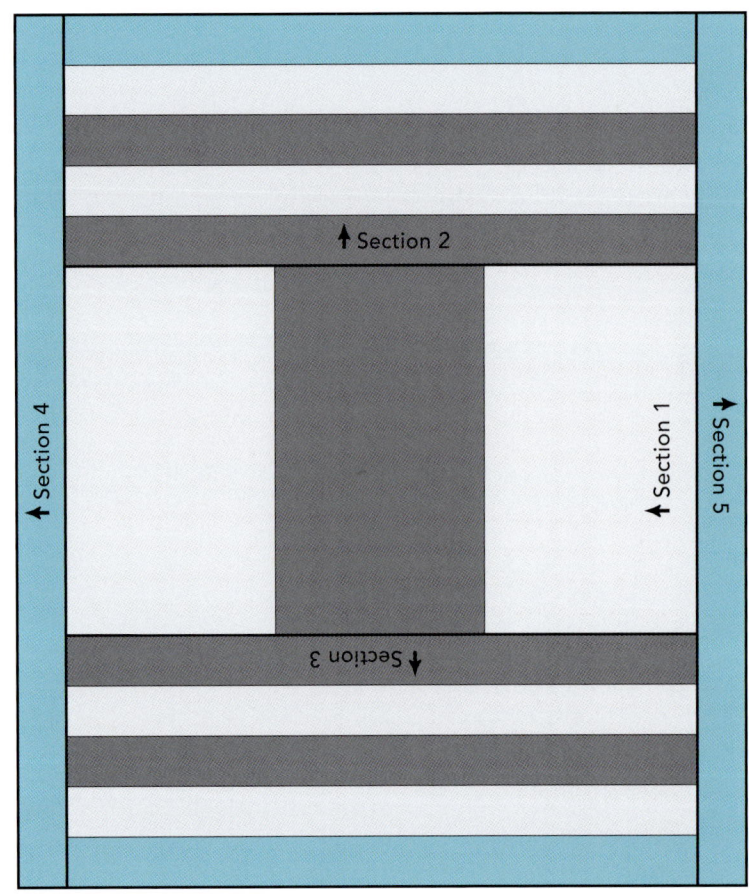

KEY

↑ direction of work

EARTHEN LATTICE PILLOW & LAPGHAN SET

Easy

MEASUREMENTS

Pillow 12 x 18"/30.5 x 45.5cm

Blanket Approx 33 x 42"/84 x106.5cm

MATERIALS

YARN

Any worsted-weight wool, approx 3½oz/100g and 190yd/174m per skein 🧶**4**

• 6 skeins in Caramel (A)

• 4 skeins Brown (B)

NEEDLES

• One pair size 8 (5mm) needles, *or size to obtain gauge*

• One size 8 (5mm) circular needle, 32"/80cm long

NOTIONS

• One 12 x 18"/30 x 45.5cm pillow form

• Yarn needle

• A piece of cardboard

GAUGE

18 sts and 36 rows to 4"/10cm over garter st using size 8 (5mm) needles. *TAKE TIME TO CHECK YOUR GAUGE.*

NOTES

1) The pillow uses 2 skeins of A and 1 skein of B. The blanket uses 4 skeins of A and 3 skeins of B.

2) The pillow is worked side to side.

3) Circular needle is used to accommodate the large number of stitches of the lapghan. Do not join.

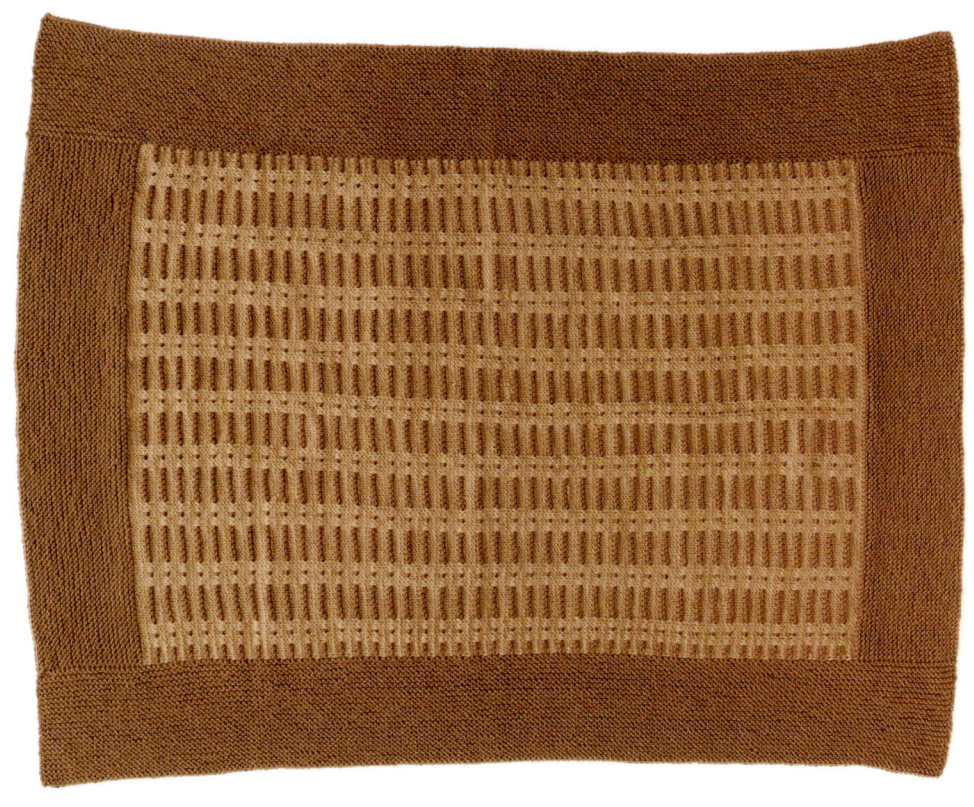

EARTHEN LATTICE PILLOW & LAPGHAN SET

PILLOW

FRONT

With A, cast on 51 sts.

Work in garter st (k every row), noting first row is RS, until work measures 5"/12.5cm from beg, end with a RS row.

Inc row (WS) *K6, M1, k5, M1; rep from * to last 7 sts, k7—59 sts.

Row 1 (RS) With B, knit.

Row 2 With B, purl.

Rows 3 and 4 Rep rows 1 and 2.

Row 5 With A, k3, *sl 2 wyib, k1, sl 2 wyib, k7; rep from * to last 8 sts, sl 2 wyib, k1, sl 2 wyib, k3.

Row 6 With A, k3, *sl 2 wyif, k1, sl 2 wyif, k7; rep from * to last 8 sts, sl 2 wyif, k1, sl 2 wyif, k3.

Rep rows 1–6 until piece measures approx 18"/45.5cm from beg, end with a pat row 4. With B, bind off.

BACK

Work same as front.

FINISHING

Sew sides of Front and Back tog, leaving one short end open to insert pillow form. Insert pillow form. Sew opening closed. Weave in ends.

TASSELS (MAKE 4)

Cut a piece of cardboard 4"/10cm wide. Wind 2 strands of A and 1 strand of B around cardboard 24 times. Cut yarn leaving a long end and thread end through yarn needle. Slip needle through all loops and tie tightly. Remove cardboard and wind A tightly around loops ¾"/2cm below fold. Fasten securely. Cut through rem loops and trim ends evenly. Sew one tassel to each corner of pillow.

LAPGHAN

With circular needle and A, cast on 101 sts.

Work in garter st (k every row), noting first row is RS, until piece measures 5"/12.5cm from beg, end with a RS row.

Inc row (WS) *K11, M1; rep from * to last 13 sts, k13—109 sts.

Row 1 (RS) With B, knit.

Row 2 With B, purl.

Rows 3 and 4 Rep rows 1 and 2.

Row 5 With A, k4, *sl 2 wyib, k1, sl 2 wyib, k7; rep from * to last 9 sts, sl 2 wyib, k1, sl 2 wyib, k4.

Row 6 With A, K4, *sl 2 wyif, k1, sl 2 wyif, k7; rep from * to last 9 sts, sl 2 wyif, k1, sl 2 wyif, k4.

Rep rows 1–6 until piece measures approx 37"/94cm from beg, end with a pat row 4. Cut B.

Dec row With A, *k10, k2tog; rep from * to last 13 sts, k13—101 sts.

With A, work in garter st for 5"/12.5cm, end with a RS row. Bind off knitwise on WS.

SIDE EDGINGS

With RS facing, circular needle and A, pick up and k 173 sts evenly along side edge of lapghan. Work in garter st for 5"/12.5cm, end with a RS row. Bind off knitwise on WS.

Rep across opposite side edge.

FINISHING

Weave in ends. Block to measurements. •

TRICOLOR LOG CABIN AFGHAN & PILLOW SET

Easy

MEASUREMENTS

Afghan Approx 46½ x 65"/118 x 165cm

Pillow 18"/46cm square

MATERIALS

YARN

Any DK-weight cotton/wool blend yarn, approx
3½oz/100g and 215yd/105m per skein 🄷

- 8 skeins in Coral (A)
- 7 skeins in Orange (B)
- 9 skeins in White (C)

NEEDLES

- One pair size 7 (4.5mm) needles, *or size to obtain gauge*

Notions

- Four stitch holders
- 18"/46cm square pillow form

GAUGES

- 20 sts and 38 rows to 4"/10cm over garter st using size 7 (4.5 mm) needles.
- 1 afghan motif is approx 9¼"/23.5cm square using size 7 (4.5 mm) needles. *TAKE TIME TO CHECK YOUR GAUGES.*

NOTES

1) When picking up stitches, pick up one stitch for every garter stitch ridge along side edges or one stitch per each knit stitch along cast-on and bound-off edges.

2) Weave in ends as you go to minimize finishing.

3) See diagram on page 36 for block construction.

4) Afghan uses 6 skeins of A, 5 skeins of B, and 7 skeins of C. Pillow uses 2 skeins each of A, B, and C.

AFGHAN

BLOCK

Make 17 blocks with A as Color 1, B as Color 2, and C as Color 3.

Make 18 blocks with B as Color 1, C as Color 2, and A as Color 3.

Center block

With Color 1, cast on 17 sts.

Beg and end with a WS row, knit 33 rows. Cut Color 1, leaving sts on st holder.

Tier 1

TIER 1 SIDE 1

Rotate work 90 degrees clockwise. With RS facing and Color 2, pick up and k 17 sts along left side edge of Center Block (1 st in each garter ridge). Beg and end with a WS row, knit 15 rows. Place sts on st holder for Side 1.

TIER 1 SIDE 2

Rotate work 90 degrees clockwise. With RS facing and Color 2, pick up and k 8 sts along side edge of Side 1 and 17 sts along cast-on edge of Center Block—25 sts. Beg and end with a WS row, knit 15 rows. Place sts on st holder for Side 2.

TIER 1 SIDE 3

Rotate work 90 degrees clockwise. With RS facing and Color 2, pick up and k 8 sts along side edge of Side 2 and 17 sts along side edge of Center Block—25 sts. Beg and end with a WS row, knit 15 rows. Place sts on st holder for Side 3.

TRICOLOR LOG CABIN AFGHAN & PILLOW SET

Tier 1 Side 4

Rotate work 90 degrees clockwise. With RS facing and Color 2, pick up and k 8 sts along side edge of Side 3, work 17 sts from Center Block st holder, and pick up and k 8 sts along side edge of Side 1—33 sts.

Beg and end with a WS row, knit 15 rows. Place sts on st holder for Side 4.

Tier 2

Tier 2 Side 1

Rotate work 90 degrees clockwise. With RS facing and Color 3, pick up and k 8 sts along side edge of Tier 1 Side 4, work 17 sts from Tier 1 Side 1 st holder, and pick up and k 8 sts along side edge of Tier 1 Side 2—33 sts. Beg with a WS row, knit 14 rows. Bind off knitwise.

Tier 2 Side 2

Rotate work 90 degrees clockwise. With RS facing and Color 3, pick up and k 8 sts along side edge of Tier 2 Side 1, work 25 sts from Tier 1 Side 2 st holder, and pick up and k 8 sts along side edge of Tier 1 Side 3—41 sts. Beg with a WS row, knit 14 rows. Bind off knitwise.

Tier 2 Side 3

Rotate work 90 degrees clockwise. With RS facing and Color 3, pick up and k 8 sts along side edge of Tier 2 Side 2, work 25 sts from Tier 1 Side 3 st holder, and pick up and k 8 sts along side edge of Tier 1 Side 4—41 sts. Beg with a WS row, knit 14 rows. Bind off knitwise.

Tier 2 Side 4

Rotate work 90 degrees clockwise. With RS facing and Color 3, pick up and k 8 sts along side edge of Tier 2 Side 3, work 33 sts from Tier 1 Side 4 st holder, and pick up and k 8 sts along side edge of Tier 2 Side 1—49 sts. Beg with a WS row, knit 14 rows for side 4. Bind off knitwise.

FINISHING

Weave in ends. Block each motif to approx 9¼"/23.5cm square.

With A, sew motifs together as shown in assembly diagram, making sure that blocks are all oriented the same way.

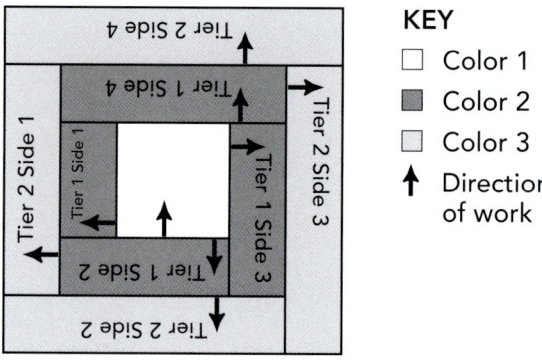

KEY

☐ Color 1
■ Color 2
☐ Color 3
↑ Direction of work

PILLOW

Note Use A as Color 1, B as Color 2, and C as Color 3.

FRONT

Center block

With Color 1, cast on 35 sts.

Beg and end with a WS row, knit 65 rows. Cut Color 1, leaving sts on first st holder.

Sides

With RS facing and Color 2, pick up and k 35 sts across left side of Center Block.

Beg and end with a WS row, knit 29 rows, leaving sts on 2nd st holder.

With RS facing and Color 2, pick up and k 16 sts across end of last side and 35 sts across cast-on edge of Center Block—51 sts.

Beg and end with a WS row, knit 29 rows, leaving sts on 3rd st holder.

With RS facing and Color 2, pick up and k 16 sts across end of last side and 35 sts across side edge of Center Block—51 sts.

Beg and end with a WS row, knit 29 rows, leaving sts on 4th st holder.

With RS facing and Color 2, pick up and k 16 sts across end of last side, work 35 sts from st holder at top of Center Block, and pick up and k 16 sts across end of first side—67 sts.

Beg and end with a WS row, knit 29 rows, leaving sts on first st holder.

Border

With RS facing and Color 3, pick up and k 16 sts across end of last side, work 35 sts from st holder, and pick up and k 16 sts across end of next side—67 sts.

Beg and end with a WS row, knit 18 rows. Bind off knitwise on WS.

With RS facing and Color 3, pick up and k 16 sts across end of last border, work 51 sts from st holder, and pick up and k 16 sts across end of next side—83 sts.

Beg and end with a WS row, knit 18 rows. Bind off knitwise on WS.

With RS facing and Color 3, pick up and k 16 sts across end of last border, work 51 sts from st holder, and pick up and k 16 sts across end of next side—83 sts.

Beg and end with a WS row, knit 18 rows. Bind off knitwise on WS.

With RS facing and Color 3, pick up and k 16 sts across end of last border, work 67 sts from st holder across top edge, and pick up and k 16 sts across end of first border—99 sts.

Beg and end with a WS row, knit 18 rows. Bind off knitwise on WS.

BACK

Work as for front with B as Color 1, C as Color 2, and A as Color 3.

COLOR KEY

- A
- B
- C

FINISHING

Weave in ends. Block to measurements.

Sew 3 sides of Front and Back together. Insert pillow form. Sew last side closed. •

SEASHORE BLANKET

MEASUREMENTS

Approx 30 x 40"/76 x 101.5cm

MATERIALS

YARN

Any bulky-weight acrylic/cotton/wool blend yarn, approx 3½oz/100g and 170yd/156m per skein **5**

• 5 skeins in a Self-Striping Sea Green and Gray

NEEDLES

One size 10 (6mm) circular needle, 32"/80cm long, *or size to obtain gauge*

GAUGE

15 sts and 20 rows to 4"/10cm over rib pat using size 10 (6mm) needles. *TAKE TIME TO CHECK YOUR GAUGE.*

RIB PATTERN

(multiple of 18 sts plus 9)

Row 1 (RS) *K9, p9; rep from * to last 9 sts, k9.

Row 2 *P9, k9; rep from * to last 9 sts, p9.

Rep rows 1 and 2 for rib pat.

BLANKET

Cast on 111 sts. Knit 2 rows.

LOWER LACE BORDER

Row 1 (RS) Knit.

Row 2 K1, p to last st, k1.

Row 3 K2, *[yo, k1] 3 times, [k2tog] 6 times, [yo, k1] 3 times; rep from * to last st, k1.

Row 4 Knit.

Rep rows 1–4 twice more.

Ridge row (RS) K6, p to last 6 sts, k6.

RIB PATTERN

Row 1 (WS) K6, *p9, k9; rep from * to last 15 sts, p9, k6.

Row 2 K6, *k9, p9; rep from * to last 15 sts, k15.

Rep rows 1 and 2 until piece measures approx 34"/86.5cm from ridge row, end with a WS row.

Ridge row (RS) K6, p to last 6 sts, k6.

UPPER LACE BORDER

Row 1 (RS) Knit.

Row 2 K1, p to last st, k1.

Row 3 K2, *[k2tog] 3 times, [yo, k1] 6 times, [k2tog] 3 times; rep from * to last st, k1.

Row 4 Knit.

Rep rows 1–4 twice more.

Next row (RS) Knit.

Bind off knitwise on WS.

FINISHING

Weave in ends. Block lightly to measurements. •

SEASHORE PILLOWS

MEASUREMENTS

SEASHELL

Width 20"/51cm

Length 12"/30.5cm

STARFISH

Diameter 14"/35.5cm

MATERIALS

YARN

Any bulky-weight acrylic/cotton/wool blend yarn, approx 3½oz/100g and 170yd/156m per skein

• 2 skeins in a Self-Striping Sea Green and Gray*

*Each pillow uses 1 skein

NEEDLES

Seashell

• One pair size 8 (5mm) needles, *or size to obtain gauge*

• One extra size 8 (5mm) needle

Starfish

• One set (5) size 8 (5mm) double-pointed needles (dpn), *or size to obtain gauge*

• Two size 8 (5mm) circular needles, 24"/60cm long

NOTIONS

Seashell

• Eight ¾"/19mm buttons

Starfish

• Two ¾"/19mm buttons

• Removable stitch marker

Both

• Polyester stuffing

• Tapestry needle to fit through button holes

• Matching cord thread or embroidery floss

GAUGE

16 sts and 24 rows to 4"/10cm over St st using size 8 (5mm) needles. *TAKE TIME TO CHECK YOUR GAUGE.*

3-NEEDLE BIND-OFF (ON RS)

1) With WS held together, insert third needle knitwise into first st of each needle and wrap yarn knitwise.

2) Knit these two sts together, and slip them off the needles. *Knit next two sts together in the same manner.

3) Slip first st on 3rd needle over 2nd st and off needle. Rep from * in step 2 across row until all sts are bound off.

STITCH GLOSSARY

inc k (knit lifted increase) Insert RH needle into back of st one row below next st on LH needle as if to knit, knit this st then knit the st on the LH needle—1 st inc'd.

inc p (purl lifted increase) Insert RH needle into front of st one row below next st on LH needle as if to purl, purl this st then purl the st on the LH needle—1 st inc'd.

SEASHELL

Cast on 20 sts.

Rows 1–7 Knit.

Rows 8 and 10 (RS) K1, [k2, p2] 4 times, k3.

Row 9 and all WS rows through row 39 K the knit sts and p the purl sts.

Inc row 12 K1, [k1, inc k, p1, inc p] 4 times, k1, inc k, k1—29 sts.

Row 14 K1, [k3, p3] 4 times, k4.

Inc row 16 K1, [k2, inc k, p2, inc p] 4 times, k2, inc k, k1—38 sts.

Row 18 K1, [k4, p4] 4 times, k5.

Inc row 20 K1, [k3, inc k, p3, inc p] 4 times, k3, inc k, k1—47 sts.

Row 22 K1, [k5, p5] 4 times, k6.

SEASHORE PILLOWS

Inc row 24 K1, [k4, inc k, p4, inc p] 4 times, k4, inc k, k1—56 sts.

Inc row 26 K1, [k6, p6] 4 times, k7.

Inc row 28 K1, [k5, inc k, p5, inc p] 4 times, k5, inc k, k1—65 sts.

Row 30 K1, [k7, p7] 4 times, k8.

Inc row 32 k1, [k6, inc k, p6, inc p] 4 times, k6, inc k, k1—74 sts.

Row 34 K1, [k8, p8] 4 times, k9.

Inc row 36 K1, [k7, inc k, p7, inc p] 4 times, k7, inc k, k1—83 sts.

Row 38 K1, [k9, p9] 4 times, k10.

Row 39 K the knit sts and p the purl sts.

RIDGE

Row 40 (RS) Purl.

Row 41 Knit.

UPPER LACE BORDER

Row 42 (RS) Knit.

Row 43 Purl.

Inc row 44 K3, [yo, k1] 6 times,*[k2tog] 6 times, [yo, k1] 6 times; rep from * to last 2 sts, k2—89 sts.

Rows 45 and 46 Knit.

Row 47 Purl.

Inc row 48 K6, [yo, k1] 6 times, *[k2tog] 6 times, [yo, k1] 6 times; rep from * to last 5 sts, k5—95 sts.

Rows 49 and 50 Knit.

Row 51 Purl.

Row 52 K3, [k2tog] 3 times, [yo, k1] 6 times, *[k2tog] 6 times, [yo, k1] 6 times; rep from * to last 8 sts, [k2tog] 3 times, k2.

Row 53 Knit.

Cut yarn and set aside on needle.

Rep from beg for 2nd half but do not cut yarn.

FINISHING

Join curved open upper edges with 3-needle bind-off (on RS). Sew side edges of cushion. Weave in ends. Block lightly.

Stuff with polyester stuffing through the opening at bottom. Do not overstuff. Sew bottom seam closed. With tapestry needle and cord thread or embroidery floss, sew 4 pairs of buttons to cushion as follows: For each pair of buttons, place at center of purl section just under ridge, on opposite sides of cushion. Pass the needle through a hole of the button on first side, *pass through the cushion to come out through a hole of the button on the opposite side, move needle to the next hole on button and repeat from * several times, sewing tightly through the cushion to create a tufted effect. Cut thread and secure end. Repeat for each purl section.

STARFISH

Note Change to circular needle when sts no longer comfortably fit on dpn.

With dpn, cast on 30 sts, leaving a 12"/30.5cm tail. Divide evenly over 4 dpn. Join, taking care not twist sts, and pm for beg of rnd.

Rnd 1 Knit.

Rnd 2 [K1, M1L, k1, S2KP, k1, M1R] 5 times.

Inc rnd 3 [K1, M1L, k5, M1R] 5 times—40 sts.

Rnd 4 [K1, M1L, k2, S2KP, k2, M1R] 5 times.

Inc rnd 5 [K1, M1L, k7, M1R] 5 times—50 sts.

Rnd 6 [K1, M1L, k3, S2KP, k3, M1R] 5 times.

Inc rnd 7 [K1, M1L, k9, M1R] 5 times—60 sts.

Rnd 8 [K1, M1L, k4, S2KP, k4, M1R] 5 times.

Inc rnd 9 [K1, M1L, k11, M1R] 5 times—70 sts.

Rnd 10 [K1, M1L, k5, S2KP, k5, M1R] 5 times.

Inc rnd 11 [K1, M1L, k13, M1R] 5 times—80 sts.

Rnd 12 [K1, M1L, k6, S2KP, k6, M1R] 5 times.

Inc rnd 13 [K1, M1L, k15, M1R] 5 times—90 sts.

Rnd 14 [K1, M1L, k7, S2KP, k7, M1R] 5 times.

Inc rnd 15 [K1, M1L, k17, M1R] 5 times—100 sts.

Rnd 16 [K1, M1L, k8, S2KP, k8, M1R] 5 times.

Inc rnd 17 [K1, M1L, k19, M1R] 5 times—110 sts.

Rnd 18 [K1, M1L, k9, S2KP, k9, M1R] 5 times.

Inc rnd 19 [K1, M1L, k21, M1R] 5 times—120 sts.

Rnd 20 [K1, M1L, k10, S2KP, k10, M1R] 5 times.

Inc rnd 21 [K1, M1L, k23, M1R] 5 times—130 sts.

Rnd 22 [K1, M1L, k11, S2KP, k11, M1R] 5 times.

Inc rnd 23 [K1, M1L, k25, M1R] 5 times—140 sts.

Rnd 24 [K1, M1L, k12, S2KP, k12, M1R] 5 times.

Inc rnd 25 [K1, M1L, k27, M1R] 5 times—150 sts.

Rnd 26 [K1, M1L, k13, S2KP, k13, M1R] 5 times.

Inc rnd 27 [K1, M1L, k29, M1R] 5 times—160 sts.

Rnd 28 [K1, M1L, k14, S2KP, k14, M1R] 5 times.

Remove marker and k first st of next rnd. Cut yarn and set aside and needle.

Rep from beg for 2nd half but do not cut yarn.

FINISHING

Join outer edges with 3-needle bind-off (on RS). Weave in ends. Block lightly.

On one side, close center opening from cast-on rnd by weaving attached strand through loops of sts with tapestry needle. Draw up tightly to gather and secure end.

Stuff with polyester stuffing through center opening on other side. Do not over stuff. Close this opening with same method as previous opening.

Place a button at center of cushion over gathers on opposite sides. With upholstery needle and cord thread or embroidery floss, pass needle through hole of button on first side, *pass through the cushion to come out through hole of button on opposite side, move needle to next hole on button and rep from * several times, sewing tightly through the cushion to create a tufted effect. Cut thread and secure end. •

FIRESIDE PILLOWS

MEASUREMENTS

16"/40cm square

MATERIALS

YARN

Any DK-weight wool yarn, approx 3½oz/100g and 224yd/205m per skein **3**

• 6 skeins each in Amber (A) and Brown (B)

NEEDLES

• One pair size 8 (5mm) needles, *or size to obtain gauges*

NOTIONS

• Two 16"/40cm square pillow forms
• Four 1⅛"/27mm buttons

GAUGES

• 20 sts and 24 rows to 4"/10cm over St st using size 8 (5mm) needles.
• 22 sts and 36 rows to 4"/10cm over mosaic pat using size 8 (5mm) needles.
TAKE TIME TO CHECK YOUR GAUGES.

NOTES

If desired, swap colors used for A and B for second pillow.

MOSAIC PATTERN

(multiple of 8 sts plus 3)
Row 1 (RS) With B, knit.
Row 2 With B, knit.
Row 3 With A, k3, *[sl 1 wyib, k1] twice, sl 1 wyib, k3; rep from * to end.
Row 4 With A, p3, *[sl 1 wyif, k1] twice, sl 1 wyif, p3; rep from * to end.
Row 5 With B, sl 3 wyib, *k5, sl 3 wyib; rep from * to end.
Row 6 With B, sl 3 wyif, *k5, sl 3 wyif; rep from *, end k5.

Rows 7 and 8 With A, rep rows 3 and 4.
Rows 9 and 10 With B, rep rows 1 and 2.
Row 11 With A, [k1, sl 1 wyib] twice, *k3, [sl 1 wyib, k1] twice, sl 1 wyib; rep from * to last 7 sts, k3, [sl 1, k] twice.
Row 12 With A, [k1, sl 1 wyif] twice, *p3, [sl 1 wyif, k1] twice, sl 1 wyif; rep from * to last 7 sts, p3, [sl 1 wyif, k1] twice.
Row 13 With B, k4, *sl 3 wyib, k5; rep from * to last 7 sts, sl 3 wyib, k4.
Row 14 With B, k4, *sl 3 wyif, k5; rep from * to last 7 sts, sl 3 wyif, k4.
Rows 15 and 16 With A, rep rows 11 and 12.
Rep rows 1–16 for mosaic pat.

PILLOW

BACK

With B, cast on 80 sts. Work in St st (k on RS, p on WS) in stripes as foll: *2 rows B, 2 rows A; rep from * for stripe pat until piece measures 16"/40.5cm from beg. Bind off.

FRONT

With B, cast on 93 sts.
Row 1 (RS) K1 (selvedge st), work row 1 of mosaic pat to last st, k1 (selvedge st).
Row 2 P1, work row 2 of mosaic pat to last st, p1.
Keeping 1 selvedge st on each side in St st and in row color as established, cont in mosaic pat until piece measures 16"/40.5cm from beg, end with a pat row 2. Bind off.

FINISHING

Weave in ends.
With WS facing each other, sew three sides together, leaving fourth side open. Insert pillow form into pillow case and sew final side. •

FIRESIDE THROW

Intermediate

MEASUREMENTS

Approx 36 x 42"/91.5 x 106.5cm

MATERIALS

YARN

Any superwash wool yarn, approx 1¾oz/50g and 98yd/90m per skein (4)

• 14 skeins in Brown

NEEDLES

• One size 8 (5mm) circular needle, 32"/80cm long, *or size to obtain gauge*

NOTIONS

• Cable needle (cn)
• Stitch markers

GAUGE

17 sts and 26 rows to 4"/10cm over garter rib using size 8 (5mm) needle. *TAKE TIME TO CHECK YOUR GAUGE.*

NOTES

1) Cables may be worked from written instructions or chart.

2) Circular needle is used to accommodate the large number of sts. Do not join.

STITCH GLOSSARY

4-st RPC Sl 2 sts to cn and hold to back, k2, p2 from cn.
4-st LPC Sl 2 sts to cn and hold to front, p2, k2 from cn.
4-st RKPC Sl 2 sts to cn and hold to back, k2, k1, p1 from cn.
4-st LPKC Sl 2 sts to cn and hold to front, p1, k1, k2 from cn.
5-st LC Sl 2 sts to cn and hold to front, k3, k2 from cn.

6-st RC Sl 3 sts to cn and hold to back, k3, k3 from cn.
6-st LC Sl 3 sts to cn and hold to front, k3, k3 from cn.

GARTER RIB

(multiple of 4 sts plus 2)

Row 1 (RS) Knit.
Row 2 P2, *k2, p2; rep from * to end.
Rep rows 1 and 2 for garter rib.

BRAID CABLE

(over 11 sts)

Row 1 (RS) P1, k3, 6-st RC, p1.
Row 2 and all WS rows K1, p9, k1.
Rows 3 and 5 P1, k9, p1.
Row 7 P1, 6-st LC, k3, p1.
Rows 9 and 11 P1, k9, p1.
Row 12 K1, p9, k1.
Rep rows 1–12 for braid cable.

CENTER CABLE

(over 19 sts)

Row 1 (RS) P1, k2, p4, 5-st LC, p4, k2, k1.
Row 2 K1, p2, k4, p5, k4, p2, k1.
Row 3 P1, k2, p2, 4-st RKPC, k1, 4-st LPKC, p2, k2, p1.
Row 4 K1, p2, k2, p3, k1, p1, k1, p3, k2, p2, k1.
Row 5 P1, k2, 4-st RPC, [k1, p1] twice, k1, 4-st LPC, k2, p1.
Row 6 K1, p4, k2, [p1, k1] twice, p1, k2, p4, k1.
Row 7 P1, 4-st RPC, p2, [k1, p1] twice, k1, p2, 4-st LPC, p1.
Row 8 K1, p2, k4, [p1, k1] twice, p1, k4, p2, k1.
Rows 9, 11, and 13 P1, k2, p4, [k1, p1] twice, k1, p4, k2, p1.
Rows 10, 12, and 14 Rep row 8.
Rep rows 1–14 for center cable.

FIRESIDE THROW

THROW

Cast on 150 sts. Work in garter rib for 1½"/4cm, end with a WS row.

Set-up row (RS) K50, pm, p1, k5, M1, k3, p1, k6, p1, k2tog, k1, p2, M1, k2, p1, M1, p1, k2, M1, p2, k1, ssk, p1, k6, p1, k5, M1, k3, p1, pm, k50—153 sts.

Next row P2, *k2, p2; rep from * to marker, sm, k1, p9, k1, p2, k2, p2, k1, p2, k4, [p1, k1] twice, p1, k4, p2, k1, p2, k2, p2, k1, p9, k1, sm, p2, **k2, p2; rep from ** to end.

BEGIN CABLE PATTERNS

Row 1 (RS) K to marker, sm, work row 1 of braid cable over 11 sts, k6, work row 1 of center cable over 19 sts, k6, work row 7 of braid cable over 11 sts, sm, k to end.

Row 2 P2, *k2, p2; rep from * to marker, sm, work row 8 of braid cable over 11 sts, p2, k2, p2, work row 2 of center cable over 19 sts, p2, k2, p2, work row 2 of braid cable over 11 sts, sm, p2, **k2, p2; rep from ** to end.

Cont in pats as established until piece measures 40½"/103cm from beg, end with a row 4 of center cable.

Dec row (RS) K50, remove marker, p1, [k2, k2tog] twice, k1, M1p, p1, k6, p1, M1p, k2, p2, k1, ssk, [k2tog] twice, k2, p2, k2, p1, M1p, k6, p1, M1p, k2, k2tog, k1, ssk, k2, p1, remove marker, k50—150 sts.
Beg with a WS row, work in garter rib for 1½"/4cm, end with a RS row.
Bind off knitwise.

SIDE BORDERS

With RS facing, pick up and k 2 sts for every 3 rows along one side edge.
Knit 6 rows, end with a RS row. Bind off knitwise.
Rep for opposite side edge.

FINISHING

Weave in ends. Block lightly to measurements. •

BRAID CABLE

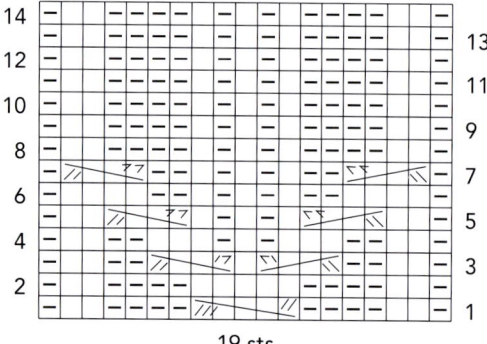

11 sts

CENTER CABLE

19 sts

STITCH KEY

☐ k on RS, p on WS

– p on RS, k on WS

4-st RPC

4-st LPC

4-st RKPC

4-st LPKC

5-st LC

6-st RC

6-st LC

LOG CABIN AFGHAN & PILLOW SET

Easy

MEASUREMENTS
Afghan Approx 47 x 57"/119.5 x 145cm

Pillow 18"/46cm square

MATERIALS
YARN
Any aran-weight superwash yarn, approx 3½oz/100g
and 150yd/137.5m per skein 4

• 19 skeins in a Colorful Self-Striping Colorway (A)

• 1 skein each in Blue (B), Purple (C), Green (D), Aqua (E),
and Coral (F)

NEEDLES
• One pair size 9 (5.5mm) needles, plus one extra for
3-needle bind-off, *or size to obtain gauges*

• Two size 9 (5.5mm) circular needles, 40"/100cm long

NOTIONS
• One 18"/46cm square pillow form

• One 18"/46cm square piece of felt fabric in
coordinating color for back of pillow

GAUGES
• 17 sts and 36 rows to 4"/10cm over garter st using
size 9 (5.5 mm) needles.

• One block to approx 9"/23cm square using size 9
(5.5mm) needles. *TAKE TIME TO CHECK YOUR GAUGES.*

NOTES
1) Blocks are worked in a tier of logs around a center
square. The cast-on row counts as the first right-side row.
2) When picking up stitches, pick up one stitch for every
garter ridge (two rows) along side edges or one stitch per
each knit stitch along a cast-on or bound-off edge.

LOG CABIN AFGHAN & PILLOW SET

3) The last stitch of the previous square or log becomes the first stitch of the next log, and counts as the stitch of the first ridge.

4) Weave in ends as you go to minimize finishing.

5) You need 2 skeins of A and 1 skein of C to make 1 pillow.

AFGHAN

LOG CABIN BLOCK

Make six blocks each with B, C, D, E, and F for center square—30 blocks total.

Center block

With B, C, D, E, or F, cast on 13 sts.
Knit 25 rows, end with a WS row.
Bind off to last st, leave last st on needle. Cut yarn.
Turn block clockwise 90 degrees.

Log 1

Join A. Pick up and k 12 sts along side of center square—13 sts.
Knit 25 rows, end with a WS row.
Bind off to last st, leaving it on the needle. With RS facing, turn work clockwise 90 degrees.

Log 2

Pick up and k 12 sts along side of Log 1 and 13 sts along cast-on edge of center square—26 sts.
Knit 25 rows, end with a WS row.
Bind off to last st, leaving it on the needle. With RS facing, turn work clockwise 90 degrees.

Log 3

Pick up and k 12 sts along side of Log 2 and 13 sts along side of center square—26 sts.
Knit 25 rows, end with a WS row.
Bind off to last st, leaving it on the needle. With RS facing, turn work clockwise 90 degrees.

Log 4

Pick up and k 12 sts along side of Log 3, 13 sts along bound-off edge of center square, and 13 sts along side edge of Log 1—39 sts.
Knit 25 rows, ending with a WS row. Bind off.

ASSEMBLY

Weave in ends. Block the 30 log cabin blocks.

Strips (make 5)

Referring to diagram for placement (see page 53), assemble blocks in a vertical strip of six blocks as foll:
With A and RS facing, pick up and k 39 sts along edge of each of the two blocks to be joined, leaving yarn attached to one. Holding needles parallel with WS facing each other and using extra needle, work 3-needle bind-off (on RS) (see page 40) to join.
Rep to add blocks to strip.
Rep for all strips.

Joining strips

Referring to diagram (see page 53) for order of strips, assemble strips as foll:
With RS facing, circular needle and A, pick up and k 39 sts along each block and 2 sts along join between blocks—244 sts. Cut A.
Rep for opposite strip, leaving yarn attached.
Holding needles parallel with WS facing each other and using extra needle, work 3-needle bind-off (on RS) (see page 40) to join.
Rep for all strips.

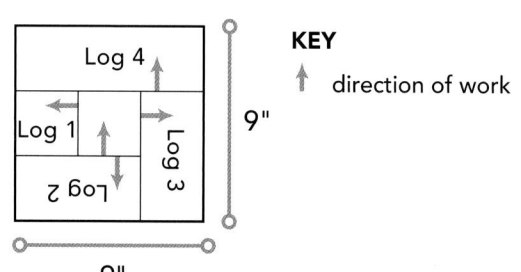

KEY

↑ direction of work

LOG CABIN AFGHAN & PILLOW SET

Borders

Note The stitch left on the needle before turning the work 90 degrees does not contribute to the block pick-up stitch counts.

BORDER TIER 1

With RS facing and B, beg at top left side of afghan, pick up and k 39 sts per block along side edge and 2 sts between blocks—244 sts.

Knit 1 row. Bind off to last st, leaving it on the needle. With RS facing, turn work 90 degrees. Pick up and k 39 sts per block and 2 sts between blocks along bottom of afghan—204 sts.

Knit 1 row. Bind off to last st, leaving it on the needle. With RS facing, turn work 90 degrees. Pick up and k 39 sts per block and 2 sts between blocks along side of afghan—245 sts.

Knit 1 row. Bind off to last st, leaving it on the needle. With RS facing, turn work 90 degrees. Pick up and k 39 sts per block, 2 sts between blocks, and 1 st per ridge of border along top of afghan—205 sts.

Knit 1 row. Bind off to last st, leaving it on the needle. With RS facing, turn work 90 degrees.

BORDER TIER 2

Cut yarn, join F. Pick up and k 1 st in each st and 1 st in ridge of left side border—246 sts.

Knit 1 row. Bind off to last st, leaving it on the needle. With RS facing, turn work 90 degrees. Pick up and k 1 st in each st and 1 st in each ridge of bottom border—206 sts.

Knit 1 row. Bind off to last st, leaving it on the needle. With RS facing, turn work 90 degrees. Pick up and k 1 st in each st and 1 st in each ridge of right side border—247 sts.

Knit 1 row. Bind off to last st, leaving it on the needle.

With RS facing, turn work 90 degrees. Pick up and knit 1 st in each st and 1 st in each ridge of top border—207 sts.
Knit 1 row. Bind off to last st, leaving it on the needle.
With RS facing, turn work 90 degrees.

BORDER TIER 3

Cut yarn, join E and repeat tier as above, picking up 1 st in each st and 1 st in each ridge of border; stitch counts increase by two sts each log. Cut yarn.
Weave in ends. Block to measurements.

PILLOW
LOG CABIN BLOCK

Make four blocks with desired color for center square. Join squares using 3-needle (on RS) (see page 40) as for afghan. Sew 18"/46cm square felt piece to knitted piece, leaving one side open. Insert pillow form and sew rem side.

Note The pillow in the photo was made with a felt backing. If desired, a second set of four blocks can be knit for the backing. •

WAVES PILLOWS

MEASUREMENTS
Breakers Pillow 16"/40cm square
Currents Pillow 18"/45cm square

MATERIALS
YARN
Any worsted-weight cotton yarn, approx 3½oz/100g and 185yd/170m per skein

Breakers Pillow
• 1 skein each in Turquoise (A) and Mint (B)

Currents Pillow
• 1 skein each in Turquoise (A), Lime (B), and Mint (C)

NEEDLES
• One pair size 8 (5mm) needles, *or size to obtain gauge*

NOTIONS
• One size 16"/40cm pillow form
• One size 18"/45cm pillow form

GAUGE
16 sts and 22 rows to 4"/10cm over St st using size 8 (5mm) needles. *TAKE TIME TO CHECK GAUGE.*

NOTES
1) Back of each pillow is are worked in a St st stripe pat.
2) Knitted pieces measure smaller than the pillow form and will stretch to fit.

BREAKERS PILLOW
FRONT
With A, cast on 57 sts.
Rows 1–3 With A, knit.
Row 4 (RS) With B, k1, *k2tog, k2, [kfb] twice, k3, ssk; rep from * to last st, k1.
Rows 5, 7, and 9 With B, purl.
Rows 6 and 8 With B, rep row 4.

Row 10 With A, rep row 4.
Rep rows 1–10 seven times more, then work rows 1–3 once more. Piece measures approx 14"/35.5cm from beg. Bind off with A.

BACK
With A, cast on 57 sts.
*Work in St st (k on RS, p on WS) and 4 rows A, 2 rows B stripe sequence until back is same length as front, end with 4 rows A. Bind off.

FINISHING
Weave in ends. Sew front and back tog along 3 sides. Insert pillow form and sew rem side.

CURRENTS PILLOW
FRONT
With A, cast on 73 sts.
Row 1 (RS) With A, k1, k2tog, *k3, yo, k1, yo, k3, SK2P; rep from * to last 10 sts, k3, yo, k1, yo, k3, k2tog, k1.
Row 2 With A, purl.
Rows 3–6 With B, rep rows 1 and 2 twice more.
Rows 7 and 8 With A, rep rows 1 and 2 once more.
Rows 9–12 With C, rep rows 1 and 2 twice more.
Rep rows 1–12 five times more, then rep rows 1–8 once more. Piece measures approx 16"/40cm from beg. Bind off with A.

BACK
With A, cast on 68 sts.
*Work in St st (k on RS, p on WS) and 2 rows A, 4 rows B stripe sequence until back is same length as front, end with 2 rows A. Bind off.

FINISHING
Weave in ends. Sew front and back tog along 3 sides. Insert pillow form and sew rem side. •

CURRENTS BLANKET

Intermediate

MEASUREMENTS

Approx 32 x 46"/81 x 116cm

MATERIALS

YARN

Any worsted-weight cotton yarn, approx 3½oz/100g
and 185yd/170m per skein 4

• 5 skeins in Lime (B)
• 2 skeins in Turquoise (A)

NEEDLES

• One size 8 (5mm) circular needle, 16"/40cm long, *or
size to obtain gauge*

GAUGE

18 sts and 18 rows to 4"/10cm over pat st using size
8 (5mm) needles. *TAKE TIME TO CHECK YOUR GAUGE.*

BLANKET

With A, cast on 143 sts.

Row 1 (RS) With A, k1, k2tog, *k3, yo, k1, yo, k3, SK2P;
rep from * to last 10 sts, k3, yo, k1, yo, k3, k2tog, k1.

Row 2 With A, purl.

Rows 3–6 With B, rep rows 1 and 2 twice more.

Rep rows 1–6 until piece measures approx 46"/116cm,
end with 2 rows B. Bind off.

FINISHING

Weave in ends. Block to measurements. •